Scotland

MYTHS & LEGENDS

BERYL BEARE

Scotland
MYTHS & LEGENDS

BERYL BEARE

CHARTWELL
BOOKS, INC.

Published by Chartwell Books
a division of Book Sales, Inc.
114 Northfield Avenue
Edison, NJ 08837

This edition produced for sale in the U.S.A.,
its territories and dependencies only.

First published in Great Britain in 1996 by
Parragon Books Limited
Units 13-17, Avonbridge Industrial Estate
Atlantic Road, Avonmouth, Bristol BS11 9QD
United Kingdom

Designed and produced by
Stonecastle Graphics Limited
Old Chapel Studio, Plain Road, Marden,
Tonbridge, Kent TN12 9LS United Kingdom

ISBN 0-7858-0537-0

Printed in Italy

Photographic credits:
(Abbreviations: r = right, l = left, t = top, b = below)

Telegraph Colour Library: 2-3, 6, 10, 29, 32-33, 44*(l)*, 44*(r)*, 45, 50, 50-51, 61, 66-67.

Colorific!: 7, 8, 12, 13, 18, 20, 21, 26, 36, 47, 51*(r)*, 53, 54, 58*(l)*, 59, 60, 63, 76*(b)*, 76*(t)*.

Greg Evans International: 1, 11, 22, 23, 24, 25*(l)*, 25*(r)*, 27, 30, 35, 37, 38, 40, 46, 51*(t)*, 52, 55, 57, 62, 65*(r)*, 66*(l)*, 67*(r)*, 68*(l)*, 68-69, 69*(t)*, 70, 70-71, 72*(inset)*, 72-73, 73*(r)*, 74*(l)*, 74-75, 75*(r)*, 77, 78*(inset)*, 78-79, 79*(inset)*.

The Image Bank: 9, 14, 15, 16, 17,,19*(l)*, 19*(r)*, 31, 32*(inset)*, 33*(inset)*, 33, 34, 39, 41, 42*(l)*, 42-43, 43, 48*(inset)*, 48, 49, 56-57, 58*(t)*, 64, 65*(inset)*.

Stockphotos: 28*(l)*, 28*(t)*.

The author would like to express her thanks to
the Perthshire Tourist Board.

Contents

Introduction

'O Caledonia! stern and wild,
Meet nurse for a poetic child!
Land of brown heath and shaggy wood,
Land of the mountain and the flood.'
 (Sir Walter Scott)

THERE can be few lines that conjure so instantly a 'mind's eye' view of Scotland. Caledonia – an ancient Roman word for Scotland – has always had the power to inspire. As one visitor exclaimed, 'the sight of those mountains makes my very soul gasp!'

The mountains can indeed be punishingly stern to the ill-prepared walker, but their ever changing moods create a beauty that is unique. When the mist comes down it is easy to believe in the existence of dragons, giants and monsters, yet when the sun shines the mountains almost smile. But beware – a Scottish magician can throw another mist upon them in the twinkling of an eye!

Scotland's scene is an ever changing one, from the softer country of the Borders – where, however, castles and abbeys may well be haunted – to the rugged wilderness of the Highlands. The whole country is abundantly rich in history and, consequently, in myths and legends. For the saints, kings, dukes and lairds of the legends probably did exist, although their stories will have changed many times in the telling.

Right: Summit of Cairn Gorm, Perthshire.
Far right: Loch Laich, near Port Appin.

Monsters, Ghosts and Ghouls

*W*HEN a Scottish loch is sparkling in the sunlight, only the most indifferent of observers could possibly doubt the existence of fairies. Yet when the waters of Loch Ness stir darkly, it is difficult to imagine there is *not* a monster beneath them.

As Scotland delights the eye, so it presents the visitor with every kind of legendary being. If you want to meet ghosts and ghouls, you probably will. But if the thought sends unpleasant shivers down your spine, don't listen for the groans in the ruined castle or look for the apparition by the abbey wall!

Many legends were born or perpetuated in poetry and song, particularly in the old Scottish ballads. Others were inspired by times of strife; riots, cattle raids and centuries of fighting between England and Scotland over the 'Debatable Land'. Now the wars are over and the raiders have gone – but the legends live on.

New area names are given with the legends in this book because they appear on recent maps and road maps and are current at the time of writing. However, many will be changing again in 1996 and you will find the original names, which I have given in brackets, used on all Scottish tourist literature.

Legends of the Lowlands

The Ploughman Poet

Alloway, Strathclyde (Ayrshire)

SCOTLAND'S best-loved poet, Robert Burns, was born in a cottage at Alloway. His father was a labouring farmer and built the cottage with his own hands. It has since been preserved as a Burns museum.

The Burns family moved from one ailing farm to another, and while Robert received a hard-won education (he could write in both 18th century English and his native Scots) his spare time was fully employed as a farm labourer and ploughman.

His poetry was prolific, of course – much of it arising from the supernatural stories he enjoyed in childhood. Some of his best work is contained in the poem *Tam O'Shanter*.

Tam O'Shanter

Alloway

IN THE churchyard of the Kirk of Alloway, Tam O'Shanter disturbed a coven of witches dancing to the music of unearthly bagpipes. The witches saw Tam and gave chase and he had to ride for his life on his old grey mare, Meg.

The fastest witch, 'Cutty Sark', almost caught up with him when they reached the River Doon. But the water rendered her powerless and she could only catch Meg's tail. Tam and his now tailless old mare managed to escape across the bridge.

Left: Statue of Robert Burns at Dumfries.

A Change Of Fortune

Anwoth, Dumfries & Galloway (Kirkcudbright)

Below: A dramatic landscape over the glacial valley of Dumfries and Galloway.

THE 15th century Cardoness Castle at Anwoth was said to be so expensive to maintain that three successive lairds went bankrupt. A fourth laird also became impoverished and had to roof the castle with heather, which he collected from Glenquicken Moor, four miles away, and carried home on his back.

Once the roofing was completed, however, the laird's luck began to change. His cattle flourished, his fortunes increased and his tenth child was a much longed for son.

The time came for his eldest daughter to marry, and a winter wedding was arranged. The laird decided that the celebrations should be rounded off with a feast on the frozen Black Loch, nearby.

Unfortunately, he chose the sabbath for this final festivity, and on the appointed day none of the invited guests turned up. Undaunted, he took his family and servants out on to the frozen loch and, after much sport, the feasting commenced.

Suddenly, there was a tremendous crack and the ice gave way. The whole family and all the servants disappeared into the loch, and were never seen again. Like the ice, the laird's run of good luck had broken!

Old King Cole

Coylton, Strathclyde (Ayrshire)

THE village of Coylton on the Water of Coyle could have derived its name from a King Coilus who was killed in battle locally, and buried in the church at Coylton. Fergus Loch, to the west of the church, may have taken its name from King Fergus, who defeated King Coel of the Britons in a nearby field.

In southern Scotland there really was a British king called Coil. By the late sixth century, the whole Roman frontier from Edinburgh to Lancashire was held by the 'sons of Coel'.

'Old Coel' himself was obviously a power to be reckoned with. But could he also have been the 'merry old soul' of the 18th century nursery rhyme? This dubious honour is usually attributed to Colchester in England, the town thought to have been named after 'King Cole'.

Some of the earliest versions of the rhyme seem to be specifically Scottish, however. One, discovered by Robert Burns, begins, 'Our auld King Coul was a jolly auld soul,' goes on to tell us that he 'fill'd a jolly brown bowl,' and ends, rather ambiguously:

'There's no a lass in a' Scotland
Like our sweet Marjorie.'

Merlin's Grave

Drumelzier, Borders (Peebleshire)

LEGEND has it that Merlin, the magician, is buried at the root of a thorn tree in a meadow a little way below the churchyard at Drumelzier.

Fleeing from a horrible vision during a battle of his own making, he begged St Mungo (originally St Kentigern) to give him the sacrament, as he knew he was about to die a triple death. His request was granted and that same day he was seized by shepherds, beaten with cudgels and stones and thrown into the River Tweed, where his body was pierced by a stake. Hence the triple death – beating, drowning and transfixing.

After his burial, a prophecy was delivered in the form of a Scottish rhyme.

'When Tweed and Pausayle (Powsail),
meet at Merlin's Grave
Scotland and England, shall one Monarch
have.'

On the day in 1603, when James VI of Scotland became England's James I, the Tweed did indeed overflow and meet the Powsail at the place of Merlin's grave.

Drumelzier is not Merlin's only resting place, however. He is supposed also to be sleeping near Carmarthen, in Wales.

Left and far left: Although not as rugged as some regions of Scotland, Strathclyde has a splendour of its own.

Thomas the Rhymer

Eildon Hills, Borders (Roxburghshire)

THERE is a tradition that the Eildon Hills formed one large peak until the wizard Michael Scot instructed his imps – Prim, Prig and Pricker – to split it into three. In fact, Eildon is really one hill with three peaks. Eildon Hill North was once the site of the largest fort in Scotland, and some of the remains of this Roman fort can be seen today.

It was below these hills that Thomas of Erceldoune – Thomas the Rhymer – was supposed to have first set his eyes on the Fairy Queen. Overcome by her beauty, he ran to meet her at the Eildon Tree and asked her to lie with him. She did so, and afterwards compelled him to go with her to Fairyland.

Thomas lived in Fairyland for what seemed like three days, but he later discovered to be three years. Then the Fairy Queen returned him to middle earth, bestowing upon him the gift of truth and telling him many prophecies, so that he became both poet and prophet. She left him where she had met him – under the Eildon Tree.

The Eildon Stone, on the easternmost of the peaks, traditionally marks the site of the original tree.

Right and far right: Steeped in history, the Eildon Hills are reputed to contain the sleeping figures of King Arthur and his knights.

King Arthur's Cave

Eildon Hills

ONE OF the many places where King Arthur and his knights are supposed to be sleeping is inside the Eildon Hills.

Canonbie Dick, a horse-dealer, was stopped one night on Bowden Moor by an old man who bought two of his horses and asked him to bring more to the same place. Dick did so, and suggested sealing the bargain with a drink, whereupon the old man led him to a cave in the Eildon Hills. Here, Dick saw stables of black horses with a knight in black armour sleeping beside each one. He also saw a table with a sword and a horn upon it.

The old man revealed himself to be the prophet Thomas of Erceldoune. He offered Dick the choice of blowing the horn or drawing the sword first, prophesying that he who made the right choice would be 'King of all Britain'.

Dick made the wrong choice and blew the horn. Immediately, a great voice proclaimed:

'Woe the coward that ever he was born,
Who did not draw the sword before he blew the horn.'

A whirlwind then cast Dick from the cave, injuring him so badly that he lived only long enough to tell his story to the shepherds who discovered him.

'Shellycoat', the Water Sprite

Ettrick Waters, Borders (Selkirkshire)

IN ONE of his earlier works, Sir Walter Scott speaks of 'Shellycoat', a mischievous water spirit who got his name from the clattering coat of shells he wore.

In the Border country, Shellycoat was believed to haunt the old tower-house of Gorrenberry, on Hermitage Water. But he could also be encountered along Ettrick Water. It is there, according to Scott, that one of his malicious pranks took place.

One very dark night, two men were approaching the banks of the Ettrick when they heard a mournful voice coming from the water. 'Lost! Lost!' it cried repeatedly.

Thinking it must be the voice of a drowning person, they followed the sound. To their surprise, it seemed to be travelling upriver. Still they followed doggedly, and continued to do so throughout a long and stormy night. Just before dawn they arrived at the river's very source and, from the opposite side of the mountain in which the river rises, they heard the voice descending.

Worn out and completely baffled, they gave up the pursuit at last. Immediately, they heard loud laughter and applause from Shellycoat, who had led them so successfully on a fool's errand!

Right and far right: The Ettrick Hills in the Scottish Borders.

The Secret Recipe for Heather Ale

Mull of Galloway, Dumfries & Galloway (Wigtownshire)

THE last home of the Picts – or 'Pechs' – was the lonely Mull of Galloway coast. They were very fond of ale, which they brewed from heather – the recipe being handed down from father to son with great secrecy.

After their final battle with the Scots, only two Picts survived, a father and son. They were brought before the King of the Scots who wanted to learn the secret of heather ale. When he threatened them with torture the father – who feared his weaker son would reveal the secret – told the king he must kill his son before he would give him the recipe.

After the youth had been put to death the father cried out that the king could do with him as he wished, for he would never hear the secret from his lips. And so the secret of heather ale seems to have died with the last of the Picts.

However, a similar recipe may have survived until recently in the Shetlands. An old woman there remembered being sent out at four o'clock on a summer morning as a child, to gather the green heather tops for a 'special reason'. Unfortunately, she no longer remembered what that special reason was!

The Soutar of Selkirk

Selkirk, Borders (Selkirkshire)

AN industrious soutar – or shoemaker – of Selkirk was always at his bench before dawn. Early one morning a stranger wearing a black cloak came into his shop. He picked up a shoe from the bench and tried it on. It fitted, and he paid for it in gold, promising to return for the other shoe before cock-crow the next morning.

The soutar was suspicious, as his customer's purse had seemed to contain worms among the gold pieces. But next morning the stranger returned and duly paid for the other shoe.

This time the soutar followed him to the churchyard, where the stranger disappeared into a grave. Later, the soutar and some of his neighbours dug up the corpse and found it to be wearing the new shoes. The soutar immediately took possession of them.

Very early the following morning the soutar's wife heard a screech from the workshop, and found that her husband had vanished.

The grave was reopened and the corpse was found to be wearing the new shoes once more – and it was also clutching the soutar's nightcap in its hand.

But the soutar himself was never seen again.

Right and far right: The Scottish Borders.

The Nameless One

Stenton, Lothian (East Lothian)

A VILLAGE near Stenton was once haunted by the ghost of an unbaptized child. Folk said the little creature, having no name, could not identify itself in the next world and was forced to haunt this one.

No one dared speak to the unhappy ghost, until a drunkard on his way home called out to it, 'How's a' this morning, Short-Hoggers?' Immediately, the little spirit rushed off joyfully, shouting, 'They call me Short-Hoggers!' And it was never seen again.

Short-hoggers are socks without feet, and folk thought this a good name for a spirit that had spent so much time wandering the district!

The Yarrow Witch

Yarrow, Borders

A YARROW youth had a terrifying nightly visit from a witch. She slipped a bridle over his head, turning him into a horse, and then rode him at a gallop to her coven.

One night he managed to overpower her and quickly slipped the bridle over the witch's head. He turned the tables on the witch and galloped her over the countryside and then took her to the blacksmith to be shod. Next morning the witch was found in agony with horseshoes nailed to her hands and feet.

It is probably no coincidence that an enduring and unpleasant nightmare was sometimes referred to as the 'riding of the witch'.

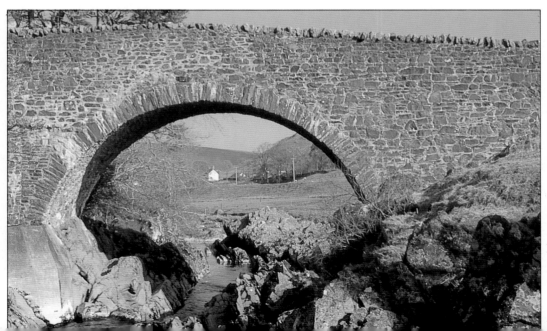

Abbeys

The Legend of Fatlips

Dryburgh Abbey, Borders (Berwickshire)

SIR Walter Scott tells the tale of an old vagrant woman who lived in a vault in the ruins of Dryburgh Abbey. After dark she would beg at neighbouring houses but always, at midnight, she would light a candle and return to the vault.

She claimed that while she was away, her home was tended by a spirit whom she called Fatlips. She described him as a little man wearing heavy iron shoes, with which he stamped on the clay floor to get rid of the damp.

After her death, few of the local peasants would enter the vault at night. It is difficult to say which frightened them most – the memory of the crazed old woman or the legend of Fatlips.

A Skeleton Danced

Jedburgh Abbey, Borders

IN the 13th century, Alexander III – a widower – chose Jedburgh Abbey for his second marriage.

After the wedding a splendid ceremony took place; a musical play was performed, masked dancers wore fantastic costumes and the whole scene was one of extravagant festivity.

Suddenly a skeleton appeared among the terrified guests. It danced towards the king, waving a bony finger at him as if in warning, and then it vanished. It was obviously a bad omen and no-one felt like continuing with the festivities.

Some few months later the king was riding home to his young bride when he and his horse fell over the cliffs near Kinghorn, in Fife, and he was killed. It seemed that the skeleton's silent prophesy had been fulfilled.

Left: The ruins of Dryburgh Abbey, supposedly the home of the spirit called Fatlips.
Right and far right: Melrose Abbey, where the grave of Michael Scot, the Scottish wizard, may be found.

The Wizard's Grave

Melrose Abbey, Borders

THE traditional grave of Michael Scot, the Scottish wizard, may still be seen at Melrose Abbey. It is level with the ground in the south transept chapel nearest the presbytery, and it has a cross on it, for Michael Scot was a cleric.

He was widely read in books of magic and was, at one time, physician, philosopher and astrologer – which was more than enough to earn him the reputation of 'wizard'. It was he who, according to Sir Walter Scott, '. . . cleft Eildon Hills in three, And bridled the Tweed with a curb of stone,' (this refers to the barrier, near Maxton).

He was also credited with the ability to fly, and of making a magical flight to Rome to visit the Pope. The Pope, presumably unaware of his unorthodox method of travelling, was amazed to see snow still on his hat.

Castles

The Laird of Co'

Culzean Castle, Strathclyde (Ayrshire)

CENTURIES ago, the Laird of Co', who owned Culzean Castle, was approached by a tiny boy carrying a small wooden can. The boy begged some ale for his sick mother and the laird told his butler to fill the little can.

To the butler's astonishment, half the contents of one of the cellar's barrels did not fill it and he was reluctant to open another barrel. However, the laird instructed him to fill the can even if it took all the ale in the cellar. The butler opened a fresh barrel and had scarcely drawn a drop from it before the can was filled. The boy thanked him and departed.

Some years later, during the wars in Flanders, the laird was taken prisoner and condemned to death. The night before his execution the door of his dungeon flew open and the boy appeared, saying, 'Laird o' Co', Rise an' go'.

Once outside the prison the tiny boy (being a fairy) took the laird upon his shoulders and, in a trice, set him down at his castle gates, saying as he did so, 'Ae guid turn deserves anither. Tak ye that for being sae kind to my auld mither.'

The Ghost of Redcap Sly

Hermitage Castle, Borders (Roxburghshire)

IN THE 14th century, the cruel and treacherous Lord Soulis owned Hermitage Castle. He had a familiar spirit called Redcap Sly, described as a horrible old man with fang-like teeth who wore iron boots on his feet and a red cap on his head. He would lie in wait for unwary night travellers, sometimes butchering them and catching their blood in his cap – hence the name Redcap.

For centuries, the hideous spectre of Redcap Sly haunted the dungeon in Hermitage Castle where Lord Soulis had held conference with evil spirits. It is said by some that he still haunts the castle ruins today.

The Mermaid's Curse

Knockdolian Castle, Strathclyde (Ayrshire)

AT night, a mermaid used to come from the waters surrounding Knockdolian Castle, sit upon a stone and sing. However, the Lady of Knockdolian found that the singing wakened her baby and had the stone broken up.

The following night, finding her favourite seat had gone, the mermaid sang:

' Ye may think on your cradle – I'll think on my stane;
And there'll ne'er be an heir to Knockdolian again.'

A few nights later the cradle was found overturned and the baby dead. And thereafter, true to the mermaid's curse, the family became extinct.

Far left: Culzean Castle, near Ayr.
Left: Hermitage Castle, said to be haunted by the evil spirit of Redcap Sly.

Cities

Jekyll and Hyde

Edinburgh, Lothian (Midlothian)

ROBERT Louis Stevenson's *Dr Jekyll and Mr Hyde* was based in part on Deacon Brodie, a character from the author's native Edinburgh. Brodie, a pillar of the church by day, became a veritable villain by night, robbing citizens in their homes and killing without compunction. He was hanged in 1788.

In the mid 17th century there was an even more notorious 'Jekyll and Hyde' character in Edinburgh. Major Thomas Weir, a respected commander of the City Guard, eventually revealed that he was in the service of the Devil. He and his sister confessed to unspeakable crimes of necromancy, immorality and dealings with spirits, and were sentenced to be burnt.

Weir was executed outside the city walls and his staff, which he claimed to be a gift from the Devil, was burnt with him. It is said that his ghost haunts the Grassmarket, and that the tapping of his stick may be heard there still.

Burke and Hare

Edinburgh, Lothian (Midlothian)

WILLIAM Burke, together with William Hare – a fellow Irishman and his landlord in Edinburgh – murdered at least 15 people and also dug up corpses to sell to schools of anatomy.

Burke was hanged in Edinburgh in 1829, but William Hare turned King's evidence and was released.

Below and right: Edinburgh Castle by both night and day.

Harry Lauder

Edinburgh, Lothian (Midlothian)

KNOWN in America as 'The Kilted Laird of Vaudeville', Harry Lauder was born in Portobello (adjoining Edinburgh on the Firth of Forth) in 1870. Each year the town presents a Sir Harry Lauder Festival, which is attended by Scots from all over the world.

To the annoyance of many Scots, Harry loved to enforce his nation's reputation for 'canniness'. When sending a hotel pageboy for a newspaper, he would holler loudly, 'Hey there, ma boy, it's Har-r-ry Lauder-r-r you're dealing with — dinna forget to bring back that penny change.' However, what most people didn't realize was that later, in secrecy, he would tip all the hotel staff very generously!

Edinburgh Castle

Edinburgh, Lothian (Midlothian)

EDINBURGH Castle, standing high on a volcanic rock, contains the country's Crown Jewels, the standards carried at the Battle of Culloden — and the room where Mary Queen of Scots gave birth to the prince who would later become James I of the United Kingdom.

Seen from the castle, to the east of Edinburgh, is Arthur's Seat. A pronounced dip between two high points of an extinct volcano, it is reputed to be the chair for a giant.

St Mungo

Glasgow, Strathclyde (Lanarkshire)

IN THE heart of the city once known as *glas ghu* (Celtic for 'dear green place') stands the great cathedral of St Mungo – its founder and Glasgow's patron saint.

St Mungo completed his religious training in Fife, in the mid sixth century. He then travelled to the house of a holy man called Fergus, who had been told he would not die until he met someone who would convert the district to Christianity. Soon after being greeted by Mungo, he died.

Mungo placed the body on a cart drawn by two wild bulls and instructed them to go to the place ordained by God. Where the cart stopped, Mungo buried Fergus and founded the church that was to become Glasgow Cathedral.

Cromwell's Revenge

Glasgow, Strathclyde (Lanarkshire)

IN 1650, Oliver Cromwell attended a service in Glasgow Cathedral. The sermon was given by Bishop Boyd, a cleric who strongly disapproved of Cromwell's politics and attacked him roundly from the pulpit.

Cromwell's secretary wanted the bishop punished, but the Protector himself favoured a more appropriate response. He invited Boyd to dinner, and ended the meal with prayers that lasted for three hours!

The Miracle of the Ring

Glasgow, Strathclyde (Lanarkshire)

ANOTHER legend of St Mungo tells of a king who gave his wife a ring which she, in turn, gave to a handsome soldier. The king was informed of this and, coming across the soldier asleep on the river-bank, took the ring from his finger and threw it into the Clyde.

Deviously, he then asked his queen if he could have the ring. She sent for the soldier, who of course was unable to produce it. The queen, now distraught, appealed to St Mungo for help.

Mungo quickly found the ring in the belly of a salmon taken from the river, and returned it to her. When the king saw the ring was safe he thought his queen must have been falsely maligned, and rounded on her accusers. The arms of the City of Glasgow still include a salmon with a ring in its mouth.

Far left: Glasgow Cathedral at night.
Left: George Square and city chambers, Glasgow.
Above: Glasgow Cathedral from St Mungo Museum.

The Casket Letters

Glasgow, Strathclyde (Lanarkshire)

PROVEND'S Lordship (1471) is the oldest surviving house in Glasgow, and is where Mary Queen of Scots stayed when her husband, Lord Darnley, lay sick in a house nearby.

Mary, already having an affair with the Earl of Bothwell, had Darnley removed to a house in Edinburgh, where he was murdered. The Casket Letters to Bothwell – which later revealed her affair with him – were probably written during her stay at Provend's Lordship.

Loch Lomond, Fife & Arran

The Fairy Stock

Aberfoyle, Central (Perthshire)

IN THE 17th century, Robert Kirk was the Presbyterian minister of Aberfoyle. He was a man devoted to study, but the country folk took his scholarly research for an unwise dabbling in the magic arts.

When his lifeless body was discovered one morning close to Aberfoyle's Fairy Knowe, word quickly spread that it was not the minister at all, but a fairy stock – a wooden image made in his likeness. Kirk himself, they said, had been abducted by the fairies and was being held in the Fairy Hill.

Shortly after his funeral, his wife gave birth to their son, whereupon Kirk's ghost appeared. 'I am not dead,' he told her, 'but a captive in Fairyland, and only one chance remains for my freedom.'

He explained that he would appear again at his son's christening, and that his cousin must throw a dirk (a small dagger) over his head to release him – 'otherwise, I am lost for ever!'

He duly appeared at the christening, but on seeing the ghost his cousin was too afraid to throw the dirk. So Robert Kirk remains in the Fairy Hill to this day.

The Glaistig

Arran, Strathclyde (Buteshire)

THE legendary glaistig was a mortal who took on the nature of a fairy, but still loved to visit human dwellings. At night she would diligently watch over the farm animals and the cattle on the hillside.

A glaistig who cared for the cattle on the island of Arran once received harsh treatment from a farmer and, much offended, decided to leave the district.

Striding out, she placed one foot on Beinn Bhuide in Arran, and used Ailsa Craig – a volcanic hump in the Firth of Clyde – as a stepping stone to the mainland! Unfortunately, as she was moving her foot, a ship with three masts passed below her, causing her to lose her balance.

She fell into the sea and drowned, and was long mourned by the people of Arran.

Above right and far right: Hills and forests surrounding Aberfoyle, Central region.

St Columba's Footsteps

Arran, Strathclyde (Buteshire)

THE caves below Keil Point contain a slab that may have been an ancient altar, but most remarkable are the prints of two right feet in the rocky knoll. These are known as 'St Columba's Footsteps'.

Near Blackwaterfoot is King's Cave, where Robert the Bruce is said to have hidden before gaining the throne. Here, perhaps, the legendary spider inspired him by anchoring its web to the cave wall – on the seventh attempt!

The Blind Piper

Culross Abbey, Fife

THERE are many legends concerning secret passages beneath castles and abbeys. Invariably these lead to underground caves or vaults – and often the consequences are dire for those who enter them.

Such a passage ran beneath Culross Abbey, and it was said that a man in a golden chair sat there ready to give valuable treasures to those who succeeded in finding him.

One day, a blind piper – possibly lured by the promise of treasure – went into the vault at the head of the Newgate entrance, playing his pipes and accompanied by his dog. The sound of the pipes was heard as far as the West Kirk, three quarters of a mile away.

The dog eventually emerged into the open air. The piper, however, was never seen again, and it was believed that he had been seized by subterranean demons.

Below: A fine statue of Rob Roy.

Rob Roy's Farmhouse

Inversnaid, Central

GARRISON of Inversnaid, a lonely farm above Loch Lomond, once belonged to Rob Roy MacGregor, the notorious outlaw.

Rob Roy's farmhouse was destroyed in 1712. The government then built a garrison fort on the site, in order to keep the MacGregor clan in check following the first Jacobite rising.

Above: Rob Roy's grave, Stirling.

The Real Rob Roy

Loch Lomond, Strathclyde (Dunbarton)

ROB Roy, in Sir Walter Scott's novel of the same name, was made into a Robin Hood type hero who robbed the rich and gave to the poor.

In truth Rob Roy, or 'Red' Robert Mac-Gregor, was the leader of a wild and ruthless clan who terrorized the district around Loch Lomond. He took up a life of banditry after losing his family fortunes, and there is certainly no doubt that he robbed the rich. This included his former employer, the Duke of Montrose, from whom he 'lifted' cattle.

He was given refuge by Montrose's sworn enemy, the Duke of Argyll, and with such exalted patronage was able to carry out his unlawful activities without hindrance.

As a sideline he ran a protection racket that would have been the envy of most modern gangsters. His clients – or victims – were tenants of the Duke of Montrose, who would pay him a percentage of their rent as 'insurance' against their cattle being stolen.

Rob Roy's Cave is near Inversnaid, and was used by his gang as a hideout and meeting place. Rob Roy MacGregor died in 1734 and is buried in Balquhidder churchyard.

Left: Loch Lomond.

The Forgetful Cowherd

Norrie's Law, Largo, Fife

THERE are two legends concerning Norrie's Law, a cairn on the northern coast of the Firth of Forth, near Largo.

The local people believed that beneath Largo Law – or hill – was a mine of gold so rich that when sheep lay on it, their fleeces turned yellow.

One day a ghost appeared on the hill and was asked by a shepherd why it had come. The ghost replied that it would appear again on a certain evening, and;

'If Auchindownie cock di'na craw,
And Balmain horn di'na blaw,
I'll tell ye where the gowd mine is in Largo
Law.'

The shepherd did everything to ensure that the ghost's instructions were obeyed. No cock was left alive to crow at Auchindowie, and at Balmain they were told not to blow the horn to summon the cattle.

At the given time the ghost appeared. But Tammie Norrie, the forgetful cowherd at Balmain, blew his horn. The ghost immediately cried:

'Woe to the man that blew the horn,
For out of the spot he shall ne'er be born!'

Then it vanished, and Tammie Norrie fell dead on the spot.

It did indeed prove impossible to move him, and so his corpse was covered by a cairn. The cairn became known as Norrie's Law, and has always been considered uncanny.

Right: A winter scene in the Fife countryside.
Below: The Forth bridge at sunset.

The Imp's Shovelful

Norrie's Law, Largo, Fife

AT THE turn of the century it was believed that Norrie's Law was made by Prig, Prim and Pricker, the 'familiars' who served Michael Scot, the wizard.

These three imps were such a nuisance that the wizard found it necessary to keep them constantly busy. So he set them many tasks, one of which was to level Largo Law.

However, they had only thrown one shovelful from the top when they were called away. The shovelful of earth landed, and became Norrie's Law.

'Roun' by the Brig'

Strathmiglo, Fife

THERE was once a Brownie living at Strathmiglo who used to cross the River Meglo by stepping stones every day, to get to the Tower of Cash.

At the tower, he would labour happily in barn and byre (cowshed), threshing the corn and milking the cows. Although he was invisible, everyone knew when he was about because they could see the work being done. All he asked for his labours was the right to help himself to any food he chose.

One morning, after heavy rain, the river was so flooded that the stepping stones were covered. The servants said that Brownie would not come to Cash that day; there was no bridge nearer than the west end of town, and they were certain he would not go such a long way round.

They were mistaken, as one of the maids discovered when her porridge began to disappear from her plate!

Asked how he had got there, Brownie replied that he had gone 'roun' by the brig', and this became a local proverb for going the long way – 'gone roun' by the brig, as Brownie did!'

Right: Remains of St. Andrews Abbey.
Inset top left: An overview of St. Andrews.
Inset top right: The ruins of St. Andrews Cathedral.
Far right: The Wallace Monument, Stirling.

The Dungeon of Terror

St Andrews, Fife

IN THE 16th century, Cardinal Beaton imprisoned Protestants in a bottle-shaped dungeon beneath St Andrews Castle. The prisoners went mad in the darkness and if their screams were heard, they were murdered.

Retribution came when Fife Protestants broke into the castle and murdered the cardinal, suspending his body over the castle wall by an arm and a leg, to form the cross of St Andrew.

Drunken Davie

Tullibody, Central (Clackmannanshire)

A POOR woman of Tullibody had a good-for-nothing husband, a smith known far and wide for his drunkenness. Nothing his wife said had any effect, and at last she could stand it no longer and begged the fairies to take her away.

The fairies flew with her up the chimney singing,

'Deedle linkum dodie,
We're off wi' drunken Davie's wife,
The Smith o' Tullibody.'

They carried her to Fairyland, where she lived like a queen. But soon she longed to be back with her husband, and the fairies took her home.

Before leaving, they gave her a magic stick, saying that as long as she kept it, Davie would never be drunk again. The story ends there, so his sobriety cannot be vouched for!

Warden of Scotland

Stirling, Fife

STIRLING Castle was captured by Sir William Wallace in 1297. Wallace was then proclaimed warden of Scotland, but was defeated by Edward I at Falkirk the following year.

Aberdeen

Burkers and Noddies

Aberdeen, Grampian (Aberdeenshire)

THE urbanized tinkers of Aberdeen lived in terror of Burkers and Noddies until quite recently. Burkers were body-snatchers and were named after William Burke of Edinburgh, who murdered several people and sold their bodies to a medical academy.

According to the tinkers, Burkers were doctors and Noddies were the medical students who helped them in their quest for victims.

At night, the Burkers' sinister black coach was reputed to leave King's College in Aberdeen and drive into the surrounding countryside in search of tinkers' camps. The Burkers and Noddies were dressed as undertakers, and bloodhounds loped silently beside their hearse-like coach. And it was said that rubber pads were used to deaden the sound of the horses' hooves.

There is a story of a travelling tinker family – man, wife and two small children – who stopped at a keeper's lodge one stormy night, for shelter. The keeper's wife gave them a drink but had nowhere for them to sleep. However, she was

sure they would be welcome at the big farm up on the hill. 'I've seen many a tramp go up that road,' she said. It was only later, on reflection, that she admitted she had never seen one come down the road again!

The family made their way to the farm and, indeed, were welcomed most warmly. The farmer's wife prepared large bowls of tea for them and promised them beds in the barn.

The tinker's wife decided to save her tea for later, but her husband drank his and immediately fell asleep. To her dismay, she was unable to rouse him, even by prodding him with a skewer. Terrified, she took the two children and ran back to the keeper's lodge.

Soon afterwards, the Burker's coach came down the hill from the farm. The keeper took his gun and hurried outside to challenge the black-coated driver. He refused to stop, however, and the keeper took aim and shot one of the horses, bringing the coach to a juddering halt. Inside, the tinker's naked body was discovered lying on the floor.

The farmer and his wife were found guilty of body-snatching, and were later hanged for their terrible crimes.

Macabre tales such as this were rife among the tinkers, whose way of life has always made them victims of persecution. At the beginning of this century there were few tinkers who would pass King's College after dark, for fear of being seized by Noddies. 'They tak' ye right inside,' one tinker claimed, 'for they want fresh bodies!'

Far left and left: The city of Aberdeen by day and night.

The Heart of Scotland

The Great Forest Destruction

Badenoch, Grampian (Inverness)

MANY tales are told of the destruction of the great Caledonian forest, which once covered a vast area of Scotland.

One tale tells of a jealous Scandinavian king who brought a hideous winged monster to Scotland to destroy the forest, because his own forests were so inferior. The creature was said to be the king's foster mother, and he set her the task of flying over the forest and flinging burning torches down on to the trees.

The monstrous hag flew high above the clouds, where no one could reach her, and spread destruction everywhere.

However, a hunter from Badenoch was clever enough to put an end to her wickedness. He got the local people to separate all the female animals from their young. This set up such a chorus of bleating and lowing that the monster put her head through the clouds to see what was going on.

The hunter from Badenoch then shot her with a silver bullet. It was a sure way of getting rid of a witch, but unfortunately it was too late to save a large part of the forest.

Right: Autumn colours light up the banks of the River Dee, Grampian.
Below: Dunnotar Castle on its rocky stronghold in the Grampian region of Scotland.

The Wolf of Badenoch

Badenoch, Grampian (Inverness)

ALEXANDER Stewart, Lord of Badenoch, was known widely for his wickedness and ruthlessness. Operating from an island fortress in Lochindorb and a castle in Ruthven, he terrorized the district and earned himself the name, 'Wolf of Badenoch'.

He was chastized by the Bishop of Moray for deserting his wife, whereupon the Wolf, who did not take kindly to being reprimanded, set fire to Elgin Cathedral and the surrounding church property.

One stormy night the villagers saw a sinister figure dressed in black entering Ruthven Castle. Creeping nearer and peering through a window, they saw the stranger deeply engrossed in a game of chess with the Wolf of Badenoch.

The stranger made a move, gave an evil laugh and cried 'Check!' Immediately the whole room was engulfed by fire. The villagers fled, and when they returned next morning it was to find the bodies of Alexander Stewart and some of his friends lying among the blackened ruins of the castle.

It is said that even to this day the Devil can sometimes be seen in the ruined castle, endlessly playing chess for the Wolf of Badenoch's soul.

The Fairy Cup

Duffus Castle, Grampian (Moray)

THERE was, at Duffus Castle, an old silver cup known as the Fairy Cup, which came into the possession of the resident family in a very strange way.

Lord Duffus had been walking in the fields near the castle when he heard a sound like a whirlwind, followed by fairy voices calling out the words 'Horse and Hattock!'

Lord Duffus took it for a greeting, unaware that they were magic words used by the fairies when they moved from one place to another. 'Horse and Hattock!' he cried out in reply.

Immediately he was transported through the air by the fairies, to be set down in a strange wine cellar. He drank deeply of the excellent wine and then fell asleep.

Next morning he was brought before the King of France, in whose cellar he had been sleeping. The king must have believed his story (or he was eager to be rid of a seeming madman) for he presented Lord Duffus with the silver cup which had been found in his hand, and then he dismissed him.

So the Fairy Cup came to Duffus Castle and Lord Duffus, now a wiser man, never again cried out 'Horse and Hattock!'

Right: A bright winter morning in the Grampian region.

'Andrew Lammie'

Fyvie Castle, Grampian (Aberdeenshire)

THE ruined mill at Tifty was once the scene of a tragedy commemorated in the old Scottish ballad 'Andrew Lammie'.

Andrew Lammie was Lord Fyvie's trumpeter, and the miller's daughter, Annie, fell in love with him. But her father disapproved of the match and forbade the marriage.

However, Annie and the young trumpeter were too much in love to heed the miller, and Andrew set off to buy his beloved a wedding gown. While he was away, Annie's father beat her for her disobedience, but the beating was too harsh and Annie died from it.

Some say that her sobs could be heard long after her untimely death. But then, the wind blows mournfully round the old mill . . .

The Curse of Fyvie

Fyvie, Grampian (Aberdeenshire)

'FYVIE lands lie broad and wide, and O but they lie bonny,' say the words of another Scottish ballad. The lands surrounding Fyvie Castle are bonny indeed, but the male descendants suffer from a curse.

Thomas the Rhymer is said to have uttered the curse against its heirs when he found the castle gates shut against him. And his prophecy seems to have been fulfilled, for time after time the male succession has failed.

Below: The Grampian coastline at dusk.

The Secret Room

Glamis Castle, Tayside (Angus)

THE 'secret room' is one of the most intriguing of many legends associated with ancient Glamis Castle, with its fairytale turrets. From outside the castle there are said to be more windows than can be accounted for inside!

The location of the secret room is unknown to anyone now, although it is rumoured that in the 19th century it was known to Lord Strathmore. Some say it must be near the old crypt, but no one can be certain.

Alexander, Earl of Crawford, was known as 'Earl Beardie' and considered to be a 'thoroughly wicked laird'. One legend tells of the night on which he was playing cards in the castle and losing heavily. His friends advised him to stop, but Earl Beardie flew into a terrible rage and swore that he would 'play until the day of judgement'.

At that, the Devil appeared in their midst and the room and all its occupants disappeared in a flash.

It is believed that if the invisible room was ever located, Earl Beardie and his friends would be discovered still playing cards, and would go on doing so until the end of time.

Left: Glamis Castle, with its fairytale turrets, is said to have a secret room that nobody can find.
Right: A moody Perthshire landscape.

'The Horse's Word'

Huntly, Grampian (Aberdeenshire)

'THE Horse's Word' was an ancient secret society centred on Huntly, and was still in existence earlier this century.

No local farmhand was a genuine 'made horseman' until he had shaken hands with the Devil. The novice would be blindfolded and taken to a barn for a 'shake o' Auld Hornie', which meant having the hoof of a live calf or goat pressed welcomingly into his hand.

Chauvinism was firmly maintained, for although the society had links with earlier witch-cults, no female witch was ever admitted!

The Mound of the Dead

Glen Lyon, Tayside (Perthshire)

LEGENDS are bountiful in Glen Lyon, including one that claims that Fortingall, at the head of the glen, was the birthplace of Pontius Pilate.

At Fortingall there was also a Bronze Age barrow which was reputed to be one of the entrances to the other world. It was known as the 'Mound of the Dead' because it was believed to contain the bodies of plague victims.

On Hallowe'en night a huge bonfire would be lit on the mound and the whole community danced round it, while young boys ran through the fields with burning torches. Fortingall celebrated Hallowe'en on the unusual date of 11 November.

The Ghost of Killiecrankie

Killiecrankie, Tayside (Perthshire)

THE battle of Killiecrankie took place in 1689. Lord Dundee waited with his men on the mountainside, to prevent General Mackay from taking possession of Blair Castle.

On the night before the battle, Dundee retired to his tent for a few hours sleep, but was disturbed by several visits from a ghost with a blooded head.

On the final visit the gory spectre pointed to Killiecrankie, below the mountain, and exclaimed, 'I'll meet thee yonder!'

The battle was fought the following day, but Dundee would not come down from the mountain until evening. It may have been fear of the ghost's prophecy, but more likely he wanted his men to have a better chance of cover at sunset.

When he eventually gave his Celts the order to advance, they responded with such fervour that Mackay was defeated instantly. But as Dundee raised his arm and pointed, signalling to his men to pursue the fleeing enemy, he was shot and fatally wounded.

Near the wild glen where he died, in the Pass of Killiecrankie, is 'The Soldier's Leap'. It was here that one of the fleeing soldiers escaped by making a precarious leap across two rocks on either side of the River Gary.

Below and right: Views over the Perthshire countryside.
Far right: The River Tay, close to the town of Dunkeld.

Macbeth Country

The Witches

Forres, Grampian (Morayshire)

SHAKESPEARE'S three witches in *Macbeth* were placed on a 'blasted heath' which was probably near Forres, although Birnham Wood was also a traditional location (see Dunkeld).

It is possible that Shakespeare had heard the story concerning the mysterious illness that afflicted King Duff of Scotland. Witches were discovered at Forres, roasting a wax effigy of the king before their fire. The witches were executed and the king recovered – only to be killed in battle shortly afterwards.

Birnham Wood

Dunkeld, Tayside (Perthshire)

ON THE south bank of the Tay at Dunkeld stands the Birnham Oak, said to be the last remaining tree from ancient Birnham Wood – made famous by Shakespeare's *Macbeth*.

While the witches in Macbeth agree to meet again 'upon the heath', their traditional meeting place is said to have been a tree in Birnham Wood.

The Seat of Kings

Dunsinane, Tayside (Perthshire)

DUNSINANE was the traditional seat of the Scottish kings, and Shakespeare's witches prophesied that Macbeth would not be vanquished until Birnham Wood should come to Dunsinane Hill. The prophecy was fulfilled when Macduff's army concealed themselves with branches taken from Birnham Wood and then marched to Dunsinane.

Recently, a much smaller enemy threatened Dunsinane Castle. According to a newspaper report, the foundations were being undermined by burrowing rabbits!

The Devil's Mill

New Deer, Grampian (Aberdeenshire)

IN THE early 19th century there were eerie happenings at Whitehall, New Deer. People swore that John Fraser, the miller, was in league with the Devil.

The belief came about because of Fraser's uncanny control over his mill. It was said that he could make the mill operate and grind efficiently without the clapper – an essential part of the machinery – and stop it at will so that the wheel could not be turned again.

However, no one seemed to know why the Devil should have given him this power.

Below: Perhaps it is not difficult to believe that water-kelpies inhabit the depths of Loch Rannoch.

An Accidental Fair

Old Deer, Grampian (Aberdeenshire)

AT AIKEY Brae, Old Deer, the usual Scottish observance of the sabbath day was disregarded once a year, when a fair was held in mid-July.

It is said that this started one summer Sunday when a wandering salesman accidentally dropped his goods in a burn. He spread them out on the bank to dry in the sun, where people returning from church paused to admire them and could not resist buying.

Needless to say, the salesman was delighted and vowed to return to Aikey Brae every year on a Sunday – which, apparently, he did.

The Haunted Moor

Rannoch Moor, Tayside (Perthshire)

DARK mountains surround the peat bogs and black waters of Rannoch Moor, the last wilderness in Britain, and it is easy to imagine why it should be associated with tales of strange creatures.

Legendary heroes and bandits as well as monsters once inhabited the region. Two of Scotland's best-known heroes, William Wallace and Robert the Bruce, used it as a base to wage guerrilla warfare against the English.

Fairies, ghostly dogs and kelpies were also reputed to haunt the moors, or lurk in the dark waters of the lochs.

A kelpie is a spirit capable of assuming various shapes and taking a delight in drowning travellers. The water-kelpie most commonly took the form of a horse, which gave rise to the belief that water horses – or monsters – inhabited many of the Scottish lochs.

One story tells of a man travelling across the moor who saw something lying on the bank of a loch and, picking it up, discovered it to be a beautifully made horse's bridle.

He took it to a local smith, who declared that such intricate craftsmanship could only have been the work of a water-kelpie.

Left and inset: Rannoch Moor, with its dark mountains and peat bogs is the last real wilderness in Britain.

For Fear of Drowning

St Vigeans, Arbroath, Tayside (Angus)

ANOTHER water-kelpie story concerns the ancient church of St Vigeans, near Arbroath, where between 1699 and 1736 Communion had never been held.

Although the water-kelpie most often took the shape of a horse, in this form he could be captured if a bridle bearing the sign of the cross was thrown over his head. And once harnessed, he could be forced to labour for his captor.

It was believed that a water-kelpie had carried the stones for building the kirk of St Vigeans, and that the foundations of the church were built over a lake of great depth. The sacrament having been so long delayed, people became convinced that if it was administered the church and congregation would sink into the lake, and everyone would drown.

Eventually, a minister decided to take the risk, watched by his parishioners from a safe distance!

The Communion without a congregation duly took place – and nothing happened. The local folk therefore considered the spell to be broken, and from then on returned to their church to receive the sacrament without fear.

Right: The countryside around Arbroath is rich with ancient myths and legends.

The Stone of Scone

Scone, Tayside (Perthshire)

THE Stone of Scone – the Stone of Destiny – was said to have come originally from Spain. It was taken to Ireland by the Scots, and years later was brought to Scotland by King Fergus.

At Scone, 34 successive Scottish kings, including Robert the Bruce, were crowned upon it, as had been the custom with their Irish ancestors. But the stone was reputed to 'groan aloud as with thunder' if anyone other than the heir to the throne sat upon it.

Some legends claim it for the biblical stone that Jacob used as a pillow. Whether this is true or not, it was certainly believed to be invested with mana – a supernatural power that can be transmuted or inherited.

The stone remained in the abbey church at Scone for almost four hundred years, until captured by King Edward I, who took it to Westminster Abbey. A prophecy concerning the stone was fulfilled in 1603, when James the VI of Scotland became James I of England:

'If fates go right, where ere this stone is found,
The regal race of Scots shall monarchs there be
crowned.'

The stone, set in a coronation chair, is in Westminster Abbey today.

Below: The Palace of Scone, with its colourful guardians.

The Wizard Laird

Skene, Grampian (Aberdeenshire)

ALEXANDER Skene was known as the Wizard Laird, and it was said that even in the brightest sunlight he cast no shadow.

He had been to Italy to learn the black arts, and after seven years returned to Skene as an accomplished wizard. People believed that he was in league with the Devil, whom he had tricked into taking his shadow instead of his soul.

There is a legend that the laird crossed the Loch of Skene supported only by his magic powers and a layer of ice as thin as the finest glass. He chose the last night of the year for his crossing, and instructed the coachman to keep the horses at full gallop and on no account to look behind him.

The carriage sped across the ice at great speed, but as it touched land on the other side the coachman could not resist looking backwards. There, seated beside the laird, he saw the grinning Devil.

The coachman fainted with fright, but the horses bore the laird safely home.

A land of legendary wizards and dragons, the Heart of Scotland is a magical and beautiful area.

Martin's Stane

Tealing, Tayside (Angus)

LONG ago, when there were still dragons in Scotland, one of them devoured nine beautiful maidens on the same afternoon.

The girls, all sisters, had been sent to a well at Pittempton to fetch water. When their horrified father discovered what had happened, he gathered his neighbours together and returned with them to the well.

The dragon tried to flee, but the villagers gave chase, led by a young man called Martin. The dragon turned north but was surrounded at Baldragon – now drained, but then a marsh – where he was wetted. Again he veered north, and again he was surrounded, and struck with a club by Martin.

As he was about to snap at Martin with his jaws, the villagers cried, 'Strike, Martin!', whereupon Martin gave him another hefty blow, which almost finished him off. He crawled away, but half a mile further on he was slain by the heroic Martin.

A stone, known as 'Martin's Stone' stills marks the spot and bears the outline of a serpent and the dragon's last words:

'I was tempted at Pittempton,
Draiglit (wetted) at Baldragon,
Stricken at Strike-Martin (Strathmartine),
And killed at Martin's Stane.'

The Great Glen

The Thorn Tree

Cawdor Castle, Highland (Nairn)

CAWDOR Castle – the scene of King Duncan's murder in Shakespeare's play, *Macbeth* – has been the home of the Thanes of Cawdor for nearly 700 years.

In the middle of the guard room in the castle tower is an ancient thorn tree. According to legend, one of the thanes was about to build a new castle and had a dream, instructing him to let a donkey laden with gold, wander about the chosen area. Wherever the donkey lay down to rest in the evening, there he should build his castle if he wished to prosper.

The perverse animal lay down beneath a thorn tree, round which the thane, undaunted, constructed his tower.

Right: Cawdor Castle has been home of the Thanes of Cawdor for nearly 700 years.

The Fairy Hind

Gaick Forest, Grampian (Inverness-shire)

A MEMBER of the MacLeod clan, serving with the Earl of Argyll as a forester, had a fairy mistress who followed him everywhere in the shape of a hind.

Argyll's officers became so irritated by the presence of the hind, that the earl ordered the forester to shoot her. The forester said he would obey, but it would mean his own death.

He fired at the hind, and immediately fell dead. As the shot hit his fairy mistress, she gave one shriek and then vanished for ever.

Below: Glencoe, scene of the terrible massacre of the MacDonalds by a company of Campbell militia.
Right: The MacDonald clan monument at Glencoe.
Below right: Glencoe Pass.

'Curse of Scotland'

Glencoe, Highland (Argyllshire)

THE savage splendour of Glencoe was the scene of a tragedy in 1692, when 40 MacDonalds were murdered by their guests, a company of Campbell militia.

The playing card, the nine of diamonds, is now known as the 'Curse of Scotland', because the pips on the card resemble the arms of the Master of Stair, who was largely responsible for the slaughter.

After the massacre, fairy pipers were said to lead Campbell troops astray in the mountains on their way back to Fort William.

The Mysterious Brochs

Glenelg, Highland (Inverness-shire)

NO RACE has vanished so utterly as the Picts. The name means 'the painted ones' and it is known from a few surviving place-names – among them the prefix 'Dun' – that they spoke a Celtic tongue.

Dun Telve Broch, near Glenelg, may be all that remains of Pictish craftsmanship. Brochs were circular stone structures, built for defensive purposes around 100BC – 100AD.

Did the Picts build them? If so, they must have possessed skilled engineers as well as great artists. But the memories of Pictish art, customs and language have now gone, and only the mysterious brochs remain.

The Well of the Heads

Invergarry, Highland (Inverness-shire)

A CURIOUS and macabre monument to seven slain clansmen stands over a spring on the Loch Oich side of Invergarry.

Alisdair MacDonald callously slaughtered two nephews who stood in the way of his bid for the chieftainship of the Keppoch MacDonalds. Retribution came two years later, when Alisdair and six of his accomplices were arrested by a posse from Inverness and beheaded on the spot.

To prove that justice had been done, the heads were placed in a basket to be taken back to Inverness. But terrifying sounds of grinding jaws and gnashing teeth were heard coming from the basket.

The heads were so obviously angry that they were dipped in the spring to cool off. The ducking seemed to work, for there were no further reports of trouble.

The place has been known as the Well of the Heads ever since, and on the monument are displayed the sculptured heads of Alisdair and his six companions.

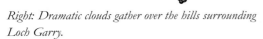

Right: Dramatic clouds gather over the hills surrounding Loch Garry.
Far right: Ancient stone mounds near Inverness.

Fiddlers to the Fairy Queen

Inverness, Highland (Inverness-shire)

LONG ago, a Pictish king built his forts on the heights surrounding Inverness, and the town has been the capital of the Highlands ever since.

Legends abound in and around Inverness. Michael Scot, the wizard, is said to have set his three troublesome demon-imps the task of building a bridge for the citizens of the town. And it is claimed that Thomas the Rhymer rests with his men and white horses at the cemetery – the hill of the yews – ready to save Scotland in her hour of need.

The Fairy Queen is reputed to have held her court in the same hill, and some say she still holds it there. Her entertainments were lavish and doubtless she was a splendid hostess. But as an employer she left something to be desired, for having paid two wandering fiddlers to entertain her guests for an evening, she kept them there for 200 years!

As soon as they ate the fairy food and drank the fairy wine, they fell into her power. They seem not to have found their stay too arduous, however, because at the end of the 200 years they thought they had only been playing for one night.

When the Fairy Queen released them and took them back to the hillside, they crumbled into dust.

The Magic Well

Loch Ness, Highland (Inverness-shire)

AN ANCIENT legend tells how Loch Ness got its name. Long ago, in the green and fertile valley, there was a magic well that supplied plentiful water for the people, as long as those who used it remembered to replace the cover.

One day, a mother was drawing water from the well when she heard her baby crying. In her anxiety to attend to the child she forgot to replace the well-cover, and the waters overflowed and flooded the valley.

The people rushed to the hills for safety, and one of them looked back at the valley and cried, 'Tha loch ann a nis!' ('There is a lake in it now!'). And so it was called Loch Ness.

Right and far right: Two views of Loch Ness and the ruins of Urquhart Castle. Reports of sightings of the Loch Ness Monster have captured the public imagination for centuries, and still continue to this day.

The Monster

Loch Ness, Highland (Inverness-shire)

SAINT Columba first encountered the notorious Loch Ness Monster when he instructed one of his monks to swim across the River Ness to fetch a boat.

The monster, who had been lurking beneath the surface of the water, was disturbed by the swimmer and darted up at the monk open-mouthed and roaring. Everyone was terrified except Columba, who made the sign of the cross and told the beast to return to its lair – which, apparently, it did.

According to this story, 'Nessy' must be more than 14 centuries old. Indeed, some people believe that there is more than one monster – and possibly a whole family of monsters – in the loch.

There have been various sightings of the Loch Ness Monster over the years, and several photographs of the beast have been taken. Sceptics have their own explanations for both sightings and photographs. These include otters, floating logs, unusual waves on the loch – and even a floating elephant!

A huge footprint was found on the shores of the loch in the 1930s, and newspapers declared 'The Loch Ness Monster is fact'. The footprint was discovered to be a hoax, but strange sightings continued to occur.

Much more recently, scientists using an underwater camera linked to a sonar unit took photographs in the deep waters of Urquhart Bay, and a spectacular photograph of the monster's head was obtained. But was this really Nessy? Or was it a model of the monster that had been left in the loch by a film crew some years earlier?

The question is wide open – and to help you decide for yourself, the Loch Ness Centre at Drumnadrochit offers a fascinating 'Monster Trail'.

The Highlands

The Legends of Smoo Cave

Highland (Sutherland)

ONE of the most impressive features of this coast is the awesome Smoo Cave, one and a half miles from Durness. In fact, there are three caves but only the largest is accessible from the road.

This is a huge, cathedral-like cavern that echoes to the drips of a burn that flows off the moors and drops into a deep pool in the second cave. According to one legend, the Devil hid in this vast chamber, waiting for Lord Reay – known as Donald, the Wizard of Reay.

Like the Wizard Laird of Skene in Aberdeen, Donald was said to have lost his shadow to the Evil One.

He met the Devil while visiting Italy, and became one of his students. At the end of term it was customary for the Devil to claim the last pupil to leave the classroom as his own. Donald got left behind and was the last to leave, but seeing the Devil about to pounce, he pointed to his shadow and shouted 'De'il tak' the hindmost!'

The Devil seized his shadow and Donald was free to return to Scotland, where the fact that he cast no shadow was frequently remarked upon. The Devil, however, did not take kindly to being tricked.

One night, Donald and his dog were walking across the moors near the sea, when a storm broke. They took shelter in the vast chamber of Smoo Cave. The dog ran ahead, deeper into the cave, and returned yelping with terror and hairless.

Donald knew at once that the Devil was waiting for him in the darkness, determined to settle the old score. But to his relief a cock crowed, and the Devil and the three witches who were with him realized that their time was up. They blew holes in the roof of the cavern, and all four flew up and away.

It is said that this is the origin of the holes through which the burn enters the cave.

Another version of the story has the Devil cornered in the cave by the Wizard of Reay, who was determined to retrieve his shadow. As the wizard was about to settle the account, the Devil blew a great hole in the cave roof in order to escape.

It would seem, from this version, that the Devil had trained his pupil rather too well!

Right: The dramatic waterfall inside Smoo Cave.
Far right: A cottage nestles on the Sutherland coastline.

Prince Charlie's Cave

Glen Beasdale, Highland (Inverness-shire)

IN 1745, Bonnie Prince Charlie – the Young Pretender – landed on the shores of Loch nan Uamh, at the mouth of Glen Beasdale. This was the beginning of the Jacobite rising, and at the end of the rising, just over a year later, he sailed away from Scotland from almost the same place.

On the other side of the loch, over a grassy beach which may be crossed at low tide, stands a single wind-blown oak. Beyond the tree lies 'Prince Charlie's Cave', and here, with a few companions, the prince hid for 10 days, awaiting a ship for France.

The Battle of Culloden had taken place six months previously, and since that time he had been a wanderer and a fugitive. Now he was scarcely recognizable; he had grown a long red beard, was bare-footed and wore a dirty shirt and plaid and a ragged coat.

Early on a morning in September, Charles and his companions were picked up by the French ship *L'Heureaux* from a cove about two miles along the coast. That was the last he saw of Scotland. A cairn marks the spot, close by the place where he had landed so hopefully 14 months earlier.

The Fairy Trinkets

Invernauld, Rosehall, Highland (Sutherland)

A YOUNG wife was pregnant with her first child and she and her husband awaited the event joyfully. But at the time of the birth the midwife declared the young woman to be dying.

Heartbroken, the husband wandered beside the neighbouring burn and hill of Invernauld, where fairies were said to live. There, he found some gold and silver trinkets lying in the grass.

Convinced that they must be fairy trinkets, he took them home to the midwife, who placed them under the young wife's pillow. Almost at once a bonny baby girl was delivered and the wife began to recover.

The husband was delighted, and decided he must return the trinkets to the hill at Invernauld.

While he was on the hillside, he discovered a cave from which the sound of music could be heard. Curious, he entered the cave – and was not seen again by mortal eyes until one year later. Then he was discovered, still inside the cave, dancing merrily to the music of fairy pipers.

When he returned home to find his baby daughter a year older he was amazed, for he swore he had not been in the cave more than a few hours.

Far left: Scottish costume at the Highland Games.
Centre left: Statue of Bonnie Prince Charlie, Loch Shiel.
Left: A sunset reflects like burnished gold in this loch.

The Seal People

Loch Duich, Highland (Ross & Cromarty)

THERE are many Celtic legends of seal-people, creatures who are able to cast off their fur skins at will and take on the likeness of humans. Sometimes they even marry mortals, but these seal-wives and seal-husbands seldom remain happy on land, for the lure of the sea is too strong.

It was said that if a mortal could steal the seal's skin during the transformation, he or she had complete mastery over the true owner.

One night, three brothers were fishing in Loch Duich when they saw the seals come ashore. The creatures cast off their fur skins and danced happily in the moonlight on the sands. Among the dancers were three beautiful seal-maidens, who so enchanted the brothers that they stole their skins. This meant the other seal-people had to abandon the three girls when it was time to return to the water.

The brothers claimed the three lovely seal-maidens for their wives. But the youngest brother was so moved by the distress of the maiden he had chosen that he returned her skin to her, and watched sadly as she swam away.

Nine nights later the seals returned to the shore and the two elder brothers locked their wives away, fearing that the seal-men would try to recapture them. But the youngest brother just watched the creatures longingly, yearning for his lost seal-love.

Then the maiden's seal-father appeared and told him that his daughter was equally in love and that, as a reward for the young man's kindness, he would allow her to return to him every ninth night.

The youngest brother was overjoyed. The other two fared less fortunately, however. The middle brother's seal-wife swam away when her children found her fur skin and returned it to her. The eldest brother burnt his wife's skin to try to prevent her from escaping also, but she discovered what he was doing and perished in the flames while trying to recover it.

Another Highland seal story tells of a farmer who saw a seal asleep on the rocks and shot it. Soon afterwards his cow died mysteriously, and various other misfortunes befell him.

He was convinced he was being punished for shooting the seal, and vowed never to harm one of the creatures again. He kept his word – and his luck changed for the better.

Above: A small boat is beached on the banks of Loch Duich, under a moody sky.
Right: Eilean Donan Castle, Loch Duich, at dusk.

The Devil Dog

Lochinver, Highland (Sutherland)

THE rock of Craig an Ordain, between Lochinver and Stoer, was reputed to be haunted by the Devil in the shape of a large black dog.

One night, a man who had come from the inn at Lochinver was on his way home along the road skirting the loch, when he heard a splashing in the water. As the moon came out from behind a cloud, he saw a huge black dog with glowing eyes emerge from the water and come up the bank towards him.

The beast growled at him, spitting fiery sparks from its mouth. Terrified, the man fled along the road, but the dog followed, and soon overtook him. It trotted in front of him, turning every now and then to look back – and the man saw with horror that there were horns sticking out of its head.

It growled and snarled at him, belching fire from its hideous mouth. Then suddenly, it disappeared through the centre of the road with a chillingly eerie laugh.

The man vowed he would never pass that way again after dark, even if it meant sacrificing his visits to the tavern.

Right: Loch Maree, whose island, Eilean Maree, was the site of pagan worship.
Far right: Loch Morar, the deepest in Britain, is home of a monster popularly named Morag.

The Island of Cures

Loch Maree, Highland (Ross & Cromarty)

ALTHOUGH Loch Maree and its island – Eilean Maree – are said to be named after St Maelrubha, pagan rites are supposed to have taken place on the island. Bulls were sacrificed and people worshipped at a sacred well and also at a sacred tree.

In the 18th century, a cure for lunacy was witnessed there. The afflicted man was forced to kneel before a weatherworn altar, and then to drink water from the sacred well before being dipped three times into the loch. The process was repeated every day for several weeks, but no report exists as to the effectiveness of the treatment.

Morag, the Monster

Loch Morar, Highland (Inverness-shire)

HALF a mile south of Morar is a thunderous weir, the site of once mighty falls that have now been tamed by a hydroelectric scheme. Beyond are the waters of Loch Morar, the deepest in all Britain. And here, a monster called Morag is said to live.

However, although there have been a number of reported sightings, Morag is not so inclined towards publicity as her relative in Loch Ness, and, supposedly, only shows herself when the death of a MacDonald of Clanranald is imminent.

The Haunted Bay

Sandwood Bay, Highland (Sutherland)

THE most north-westerly beach in Britain, Sandwood Bay, is haunted by a mermaid. There is seldom anyone to be seen in this great, lonely bay where the waves rush constantly shorewards. But Sandy Gunn, a shepherd, had an encounter with the mermaid herself.

She had been stranded by the tide on a ledge of rock and Sandy, who was walking his dog along the shore, had a chance to get a good look at her. She had auburn hair and green eyes, and but for her fishy tail and arched back, could have been taken for a lovely mortal girl.

Sandy and the mermaid stared at each other in surprise, and then the dog gave a terrified howl and rushed up the beach as if pursued by the Devil. Sandy himself was suddenly aware of what he was seeing and also took fright. Like the dog, he fled up the beach and away.

The mermaid has been seen many times since, in and around the bay. Sometimes she is completely visible, but more often it is only her red hair that can be seen, swirling below the surface of the waves.

Right: Rugged cliffs along the Sutherland coastline.
Right inset: A stormy sky broods over Loch Glendhu.
Far right: A magnificent Highland deer.

The Storm Witch

Scourie, Highland (Sutherland)

SOME Highland witches are said to control the weather. They are called Storm Witches and are capable of raising great hurricanes and snow storms, or of calming the waves at will.

Such a witch lived at Scourie, and made a good living by selling favourable winds to mariners, few of whom would set sail without first consulting her. She would stand on a rock above Scourie Bay, pointing her staff in the direction of the wind she wanted to invoke. Then she would chant a *geasan* (a Gaelic spell) and the tempest would commence – or cease, according to her wish.

One day, the master of a vessel visited her, asking for an east wind with which to set sail. She obtained it for him, but he refused to pay her, laughing scornfully and declaring that the wind had been about to change anyway.

She allowed him to set sail, but as soon as his vessel was some distance from the shore she changed the direction of the wind, so that he was swept back into the bay and stranded on the rocks.

Humiliated and chastized, the master swore never to try to trick a Storm Witch again.

The Healing Loch

Strathnaver, Highland (Sutherland)

LOCH na Naire has long been famed for its curative properties. The magic powers of the loch were thought to be at their greatest at midnight on the first Monday in August. They were also thought to be very effective during the May festival of Beltane.

On both these occasions people flocked to the banks of the loch and cast coins and trinkets into the water. This was said to date back to pagan times, when part of the healing ritual was the offering of gifts to the loch waters.

However, in a later story the loch is reputed to have got its powers from a magic charm stone, owned by an old woman.

A young Highlander, one of the Gordons of Strathnaver, tried to take the stone from her, but she refused to part with it. He then attempted to drown her in the loch and take the stone by force. But she threw it far out into the water and cried, 'May this stane do good to all – except a Gordon of Strathnaver!'

The waters closed over her head – and thereafter Loch na Naire became a healing loch.

Above: The stirring sight, and sound, of a colourful Highland piper.
Right: The twin peaks of Suilven disappear into clouds.
Far right: Highland cattle are well prepared for cold Scottish winters, with their thick, shaggy coats.

Where the Devil Washes

Strathpeffer, Highland (Ross & Cromarty)

THE hot sulphur springs and iron springs which are found in this area are thought to be used by the Devil.

In places, these two waters mingle as they flow, and wherever they do so, they run black. This, people say, is where the Devil constantly washes himself and his black clothes.

Other local legends concern the 16th century Braham Seer and his prophecies. In the first of these he said that when five church spires should rise in Strathpeffer, ships would sail over the village.

The inhabitants have always been aware that their land could be flooded by the Cromarty Firth, so when a fifth church was proposed at the beginning of this century, they strongly objected.

The church was built and no disaster occurred. However, just after the First World War an airship flew over the village, and the prophecy was considered to be fulfilled.

The ruined Braham Castle, nearby, was once the home of the Seaforth family. Their extinction was predicted by the Braham Seer, who said that the last earl would see all his sons die before him. Many years later this did, in fact, happen.

The Legends of Skye

The Haunted Hills

Cuillin Hills, Isle of Skye

THE Black and Red Cuillins form one of the most spectacular areas of Skye, and they abound in legendary tales.

Wild and towering beyond Sligachan Burn, they are said to be haunted by the ghost of an outlaw called MacRaing, who robbed and murdered a young woman.

When his son threatened to expose him, MacRaing killed him too. He then severed his head from his body, and dropped it in an old well by Loch Slapin, south of the Cuillins. The well is now called Toba a Chinn – the well of the head.

Loch Coruisk, in the Black Cuillins, is supposed to be the home of a kelpie who, like many of its kind, frequently takes the shape of a monstrous water-horse.

In the Red Hills, there are still memories of Skye's ancient Viking rulers. The remains and all the treasure of a 13th century Norwegian princess are buried beneath a cairn on Beinn na Caillich. She said she wanted the winds of Norway to blow over her grave.

More materialistic, however, was a Danish princess, who stretched a chain across the water to the mainland and took a toll fee from every ship wishing to pass.

The Tables Turned

Duntulm Castle, Isle of Skye

DUNTULM Castle, the ancient seat of the Lords of the Isles, was once the subject of great rivalry between the young MacDonald, son of the late Chief, and his cousin Angus.

Both men claimed a right to the title and the castle. Young MacDonald had the popular vote, but Angus had the love of Margaret, ward of the late Chief.

Together they planned to overthrow Mac Donald. Angus and his men would come to the castle silently by night, block up every exit with stones and then dig at the foundations until the castle fell, burying their enemies beneath it.

However, one of MacDonald's servants overheard the plot and reported it to his master. On the night that Angus and his men crept noiselessly towards the castle, they were greeted by MacDonald's own men – well armed and prepared.

Angus was taken prisoner and marched before his cousin, who had him escorted to the top of the castle and locked in a tiny room. There, to his horror, he heard the sound of masons blocking up the door from the outside.

Only after the MacDonalds had abandoned the castle, many years later, was the room opened and his skeleton discovered.

All pictures: The spectacular Cuillin Hills on the Isle of Skye abound in legendary tales.

The Fairy Flag

Dunvegan Castle, Isle of Skye

THE famous Fairy Flag of the MacLeods is now displayed in the drawing-room of Dunvegan Castle. There are a great many legends concerning the flag and how it came to Dunvegan – the stronghold of the MacLeods since the 13th century.

King Harald of Norway set out to conquer England in 1066, carrying a magic flag called Land-Ravager, which was guaranteed to bring victory to its owner. But the Norwegian army was defeated at Stamford Bridge in Yorkshire, and their king was killed on the battlefield.

Land-Ravager, which seems not to have fulfilled its promise on this occasion, vanished. The MacLeods of Dunvegan trace their ancestry back to the Norse King Harald, so there is just a possibility that Land-Ravager and the Fairy Flag are one and the same.

More romantic, is the story that the flag was given to an ancestral MacLeod by his fairy wife. It was said to be a parting gift to her husband, when she returned to Fairyland after 20 years of marriage. The place where they parted, near Dunvegan, is known still as Fairy Bridge.

Whenever the MacLeods are in peril in battle, if they unfurl the Fairy Flag it is said that they will be victorious. They can only exert the magic three times, however, and it has already been used twice. Once at the Battle of Glendale in 1490 and again at Trumpan in 1580 – both times bringing victory.

There is also a song, *The Dunvegan Lullaby*, associated with the Fairy Flag. In the 15th century the wife of a chieftain known as Surly John gave birth to a baby boy. A fairy came to the castle and searched for the tiny heir. She found him, took him on her knee and sang *The Dunvegan Lullaby* to him. Then she wrapped him in the Fairy Flag and put him back in his cradle.

The baby's nurse had watched this, too amazed to speak. But she remembered the words and music of the lullaby after the fairy had left, and sang them to the baby whenever she wanted to soothe him.

It became a tradition for ever afterwards that only women who knew the fairy's song would be appointed as nurses to the MacLeod heirs.

Above: Dunvegan Castle – the stronghold of the MacLeods since the 13th century.
Right: The landscape around Dunvegan.

The Headless Body

Staffin, Isle of Skye

THERE are many legends in this part of Skye – and some of them are macabre. A particularly nasty ghost called Colann gun Cheann – known as 'The Headless Body' – used to stun and murder people in the Trottenish area by flinging his head at them. At one time, he left Skye and continued his diabolical habit in Arisaig, on the mainland, where victims were more numerous.

He finally met his match when a young soldier caught the head on the point of his sword, and returned it only on condition that the ghost returned to Skye.

The Loch of Heads at Cuidrach, Trotternish, is the source of yet another ghoulish story.

A group of MacDonalds were said to have decapitated the MacLeods whom they defeated. Then they rolled the heads down a hill and into the loch. As the heads tumbled downhill they cried out, 'Almost! We almost won today!' Ever since, the hill has been known as Almost Hill.

There is a tradition of witchcraft in the area, too. A local laird who persecuted witches was drowned in a terrible storm – raised, it is said, by all the Storm Witches of Scotland.

Right inset: The Old Man of Storr, Isle of Skye.
Right: Loch Leathan, with the Old Man of Storr silhouetted on the distant hillside.

The Stone Couple

Old Man of Storr, Isle of Skye

THE two natural stone pillars, five miles north of Portree, are said to be man and wife. But they now make an odd couple, because the wife has fallen over.

Once, however, the two great rocks stood upright, side by side. Some say they were an old couple who had lost their cow and went looking for it, and while searching they encountered some giants and fled from them. However, they made the mistake of looking back – and were turned to stone on the spot.

The Spirit of the Loch

Strath, Isle of Skye

A LOCH near the church of Cill Chriosd was cleared of evil spirits by St Columba, when he visited the island in 570AD.

Later, however, the loch became the haunt of a wicked water-kelpie that appeared in the shape of a handsome young man. In this guise it would abduct and seduce young women, and gallop off with them into the loch.

One day, by mistake, it seized upon a priest in long flowing robes, and, protected from the evil spirit by his calling, the priest took the opportunity of converting the 'young man' to Christianity.

The water-kelpie has never been known to trouble the district since.

Above: The Skye coastline.

Mull, Iona & Islay

Royal Bones

Iona

THIS little island, with its impressive Benedictine Abbey, lies just across the Sound of Iona from Mull.

St Columba chose Iona as the starting point for his mission to establish Christianity in Scotland, in the sixth century. Here, he and his followers constructed the primitive buildings of turf and stone that formed the basis of the first church in Scotland.

Reilig Odhrain, the graveyard named after a brother of St Columba, is said to contain the bones of 48 Scottish kings. They range from Kenneth MacAlpine, who united Scots and Picts, to the 11th century usurper who inspired Shakespeare's play *Macbeth*.

Princess Ile

Islay

THE island of Islay, south of Mull and south-west of Jura, is said to have taken its Gaelic name – Ile – from a Danish princess.

Princess Ile made her way there from Ireland, stepping carefully on stones that formed magically for her in the water as she walked.

Ironically enough, although she seems to have made this precarious crossing safely, she later drowned while swimming just off the shore. Her grave is marked by a standing stone above Knock Bay, and according to the legend it is enchanted – anyone attempting to open it is destined to go mad.

Below left: Celtic cross standing proudly at Iona Abbey.
Below: The sunset over Iona, from the Isle of Mull.
Right: The town of Tobermory — according to legend, one
of the ships from the Spanish Armada was destroyed in
Tobermory Bay.

The Galleon Disaster

Tobermory, Mull

THE *Florencia*, a ship of the Spanish Armada, was reported to have been destroyed in Tobermory Bay. There are various legends as to how the tragedy occurred, and one of them starts with a dream.

Viola, daughter of the King of Spain, dreamt of a man from far off Mull, and sailed to the island to meet her dream lover. She recognized him at once as MacLean, Chief of the Clan Duart.

Unfortunately, MacLean already had a wife — and she was extremely jealous. As soon as she realized Viola's intentions, she ordered the ship to be blown up. The destruction took place and everyone on board perished except the cook, who was blown to Strongarth, where he remained.

Viola was buried at Lochaline and her father, hearing of the tragedy, sent a Captain Forrest with another ship to avenge the loss.

As soon as the ship dropped anchor, MacLean's wife summoned every Storm Witch on Mull to her aid. The witches disguised themselves as seagulls and raised a terrible storm, in which Captain Forrest's vessel sank off Tobermory Bay.

Legends of the Western Isles

The Ivory Images

Loch Resort, Lewis

MANY years ago, a murderous herdsman lived on the shores of Loch Resort. When, one day, a shipwrecked sailor swam ashore the herdsman showed him no mercy, but murdered him for the bundle he carried.

On opening the bundle, he discovered that it contained a number of little images carved from ivory. Thinking they must be the sailor's gods, he became frightened and buried them.

The herdsman was eventually hanged for another murder, and just before dying he confessed to burying the little figures. However, his listeners were superstitious and decided not to disturb them. It was not until 1831 that they were rediscovered and recognized as a set of ancient chessmen.

The famous Lewis Chessmen are believed to represent a medieval Viking army, at a time when even bishops were expected to enter battle.

The Blue Men of the Minch

The Minch

THE Shiant Isles lie in the Minch, the sea channel between Lewis and the Scottish mainland. They are known as the 'Charmed Isles', but it is said that storm-kelpies make the seas surrounding them constantly turbulent.

The blue figures of the kelpies with their bearded faces may still be seen bobbing in the waves between the Shiant Isles and Lewis, a tideway known as the 'Stream of the Blue Men'. Here, they were said to attack passing vessels and lure the crews to their doom in undersea caves.

Death and the Only Son

Vatersay and Barra

THE cockerel is regarded as an averter of evil, and if it was heard to crow at midnight, it was thought to be a sign of good fortune approaching. But on Barra, a huge white speckled bird is said to live and screech repeatedly at night if bad luck or evil is imminent.

It was a tradition that many old families of the Highlands and Islands had their particular death omens, which came to them in the shape of a bird and screeched horribly.

South of Barra is the little island of Vatersay, where an old woman lived with her only son. She always said that if Death came to claim him, she would go in his place. Her constant cry of 'Death, Death – do not take the only son!' irritated the villagers to such an extent, that they decided to put her to the test.

They plucked a live hen and threw it into her house. One of the boys then cried out, 'Old hag, old hag – here is Death come for you!' and gave a horrible screech.

Terrified, the old woman called back, 'Death, Death – take the only son and leave me in peace!'

Far left: The Isle of Lewis.
Left top: The ancient Stone circle at Callanish, Lewis.
Left: Sunset over the Western Isles.

Shetlands & Orkney

Bed for a Giant

Dwarfie Stane, Hoy and Gramsay, Orkney

ON THE island of Hoy stands a huge block of sandstone, into which a burial chamber was cut in about 2000BC.

This is the Dwarfie Stane, and Sir Walter Scott seemed to think that the owner of the stone, sometimes seen sitting by it, was a dwarf or 'trow' (troll). He may well have been right, for the trow is very common in Orkney folk tradition.

However, the local people believed that the stone was occupied by a giant and his wife. It was thought that a space cut out in the stone was their bed, and a hole above it their chimney.

If the inhabitants were giants, they must have been very cramped. A dwarf would certainly fit in to the stone more comfortably.

All pictures: The Shetland Islands abound with myths and legends of giants, trolls and sea creatures.

The Troll Stones

Haltadans, Fetlar, Shetlands

THE Haltadans – a circle of stones with two stones in the centre – are believed to be trolls who frequently danced there by moonlight.

They once made the mistake of dancing until dawn, and were turned to stone as a punishment. The two stones at the centre are said to be the fiddler and his wife.

A Tale of the Sea-trow

Ve Skerries, Shetlands

SEA-trows are human-like creatures that live in the ocean. They wear seal-skins in order to come ashore and, like seal-people, if they lose their skins they cannot return to the sea.

One of their particular land haunts were the Ve Skerries, north-west of Papa Stour.

One day, some fishermen landed there and stunned and skinned several seals, leaving them senseless on the rocks. A tremendous swell arose as the fishermen were about to leave, and in the rush to get away, one man was left behind.

Soon after, a number of seals came ashore, stripped off their skins and revealed themselves to be sea-trows. They quickly revived the stunned seals, who were also sea-trows and much saddened by the loss of their skins, without which they could never return home.

The mother of one of the sea-trows promised the fisherman that she would carry him back to Papa Stour, if he would bring her the seal-skin belonging to her son, and he agreed.

Once at Papa Stour he gave the mother all the skins, so that not only her son but the other sea-trows, too, could return to their ocean homes.

Index & Place Names